## About the Author

Ana Sofia Lara is a twenty-one-year-old student, based in Mexico City, Mexico. She is currently enrolled in a fashion major after dropping out of law school, which she attended for two years. Her passions have been reading, writing and painting for as long as she can remember, although her enthusiasm for poetry started when she read the work of William Blake in high school. She hopes to continue developing and working on her creative side from now on.

cover art by Andrés Maldonado

# Of Moondust and Hope

# Ana Sofia Lara

# Of Moondust and Hope

Olympia Publishers
*London*

**www.olympiapublishers.com**
OLYMPIA PAPERBACK EDITION

Copyright © Ana Sofia Lara 2020

The right of Ana Sofia Lara to be identified as author of this work has been asserted in accordance with sections 77 and 78 of the Copyright, Designs and Patents Act 1988.

**All Rights Reserved**

No reproduction, copy or transmission of this publication may be made without written permission. No paragraph of this publication may be reproduced, copied or transmitted save with the written permission of the publisher, or in accordance with the provisions of the Copyright Act 1956 (as amended).

Any person who commits any unauthorised act in relation to this publication may be liable to criminal prosecution and civil claims for damage.

A CIP catalogue record for this title is available from the British Library.

ISBN: 978-1-78830-677-5

This is a work of fiction.
Names, characters, places and incidents originate from the writer's imagination. Any resemblance to actual persons, living or dead, is purely coincidental.

First Published in 2020

Olympia Publishers
Tallis House
2 Tallis Street
London
EC4Y 0AB
Printed in Great Britain

# Dedication

For those who have always truly seen me and believed in me.

he kissed me stupid. he kissed me to the point where every cell in my body was thinking about that kiss instead of functioning properly. the only cells in my body that seemed to work were the ones that commanded my nerves to form a smile on my face. that smile too, was thinking about the kiss.

and so I held his hand
when all I wanted to do
was hold yours
and while he and I
interlaced fingers
I imagined
they were yours

I wonder what you say
when they ask of me
I don't even know
if you know enough about me
to actually say something

I'm like a record you bought
but never got around to play

it's funny isn't it?
how I'm completely yours
but you'll never be mine

here I am
in front of him
wishing I could fall for him
but how could I?
I haven't fallen out of you

it's actually harder
getting over something
that never happened

instead of being something that was
it's everything it couldn't be

almost anyone
can alter your hormones
notice the people
that alter your neurons

I write these words
as if putting them on paper
will get you out of my head

yesterday
I dreamt of you and me
not us

you and me
separately

as we are
unfortunately
as we'll always be

the night we met
the stars sighed in relief
for a moment there
they didn't think
we'd find our way
to each other

how could we ever be together?
we're filled different ways

me so full of love
you so full of shit

shouldn't have asked around
shouldn't have learned your name
now it lingers around in my brain
now I can't get you out of my head

it's been so long
I don't think
I know the difference anymore
between wishing to be loved
or just wanting attention

the idea of holding hands
being romantic
has got to be
the purest form of desire

I need to stop romanticizing
the way we stare at each other
if you were interested
you would've done something

there's no point in fooling myself
if something was meant to happen
it already would've
because as much as I believe in fate
and letting things take their course
you were the one
that had a choice to make

it's such an accurate description
your heart dropping to your stomach
I took anatomy classes
I know it's not possible
but that's what happens
whenever your name comes up

I used to feel butterflies
illusion of the love we could share
the love I could give to you

and now I feel
my heart dropping to my stomach
regret from what didn't happen
sadness for what couldn't be

pick yourself up darling
I know you feel out of love
but you contain a universe

it's blinding for most people
it might be too much
for the people you want to show it to

but along will come the person
who will appreciate your universe
who will give you theirs too

maybe it's my fault
for holding you up
to such a high standard

it's in your nature
and it's in mine
you were bound to ruin it

it's easy to ruin something
that seems perfect
when our nature
is to be messy and human

I've never been so disappointed
and yet I blame myself
for thinking you were perfect

give me a chance
to follow my heart
in case it leads to yours

give us a chance
to see if what we have
can be love

I wish I knew
you still think
about me too
maybe then
we could meet
halfway

you have a hold over me
I don't quite understand

electricity flows in the air
you look at me and I look away

it sends a shiver through my being
to imagine your hand on my body

it seems so unfair
to feel all this heartache
without getting to feel
all the love

what is the process?
how does it work?
I write about you
to cleanse myself
to get you out of my head
but all this does
is make me think about you
makes you linger longer in my mind

this process I'm trying out
doesn't seem to be working
I catch myself
thinking about the perfect words
to describe the way
I feel about you
I'm supposed to feel lighter
but all I feel is nostalgia

I don't believe
it's a coincidence
I was waiting
for the clock
to strike 11:11
so that I could make a wish
and I forgot about it
while talking to you

it's hard to find a balance
between not losing my head
over the possibility of us
and fighting what I feel
when I feel it all over

the idea of someone wanting
all this love I'm ready to give
is so unknown to me

I'm scared it'll come out flowing
and leave me empty
(but overflow you)

I'm also excited
you'd have the chance
to be the first
the first of almost everything

finding a balance
never seemed so hard

I can feel my heart pounding
eager to jump out of my chest
and into your hands
eager to cross paths with yours
as it jumps into mine

the idea of you hating me
makes me want to cry
unfortunately
I don't even think I'm that relevant
I think I was just a possibility
and I became a disappointment

blinded by rage
and looking to hurt you
I drove a wedge between us
that wedge turned into a black hole
it sucked everything in between
left nothing alive

I was looking to hurt you
and hurt both of us instead

humans have a funny nature
we feel so deeply
we care so very much

yet we're willing
to give up everything
for momentary pleasures

it's driving me crazy
to "let things flow"
to try and stay calm
when all I want to do
is walk right up to you
and kiss you
to walk right up to you
and give you everything
to let you know I'm ready
ready to be there for you
whenever you let me
and if you'll let me
maybe forever

I love people
who are themselves
unapologetically

they remind me
of the ocean
of lightning
of a forest
of a burning sky
of so much of everything
it just spills over

so much beauty
but most importantly
so much life

they can't help it
there are galaxies inside them
and they're willing
to share it with those around them
they let their light shine onto others

there's nothing more beautiful
than someone who spills over
there's nothing more beautiful
than an unapologetic person

you smile and I melt
I like to think of myself as cold
always being able to keep my cool
cold as the iceberg that sunk the Titanic

but you smile and I melt
I'm not the iceberg, I'm the boat
I sink into you
I fall into your depth

I don't think I'll ever be able
to reach the surface again
I don't know if I want to

have a movie-like moment
have a life changing realization
change your mind as I walk away

run up to me and tell me
you realized you can't live without me
that you don't care about the odds
that not holding my hand drives you crazy

embrace me and then kiss me
as we both realize we've stumbled
into something a lot like magic
that we don't want to let go

don't compare yourself
with the rest of the world

a planet cannot
be compared
to a galaxy

I think I could spend a lifetime
trying to forget
the way you make me feel

the way my heart pounds
when we make eye contact
the way my hands sweat
when my foot brushes against yours
the way I lose my mind
when you smile at me

you are the bravest of them all
you fought a battle
he wouldn't even know how to fight
you came out victorious

his hands aren't etched into your skin
your cells regenerate themselves
over the course of time
you will one day have a body
he will have never touched

he's the one that has to avoid you
he will be the one to lose sleep
not the other way around

I know seeing him takes you back
to such an awful place
but change the perspective
change the narrative
you're a warrior
you're wounded
not broken
he's the coward
not you
he's the one that should hold back tears
when he thinks about that night

one day you'll realize
he's the one that should be frightened
when he hears your footsteps

I felt so foolish
yet so accomplished

I saw your name
and it meant nothing
the idea of you
officially became numb

I grinned from ear to ear
I knew this day would come

I imagine you
imagining me
this is how
I fall asleep
every night

I sigh in relief
it turns out
I'm not
permanently damaged

my therapist told me
I think of him
and not of you
because I think you're foolish
for liking someone like me

I crave his approval
because I fear rejection
I don't imagine myself with you
because I don't love myself

and now that I know
I can change it
now that I know
the root of my problem
I can rip out
this poisonous vine
of lack of self-love

my favorite thing in the world
are sunsets
I'll know I have found the one
when I'm staring at the sunset
and all I want to do
is share it with them

maybe I should have kissed you back

maybe everything would be different
if I hadn't turned away

maybe maybe maybe

guess we'll never know

imagine
me and you
I know
I do

I'll be here while you make up your mind
it's not a matter of if
it's a matter of when

we're destined you see
we'll happen one way or another
so I'll be here

I won't pause my life for you
but I'll drop everything if you ask me to
correction – when you ask me to

I wish
we were lovers

that way
you wouldn't have
to look away
whenever I catch you
glancing at me

if we were lovers
we could stare
into each other
for eternity

I really hope you're not the one

I hope you're not the one
I spend the rest of my life with

what would we tell the kids?
how could I tell our son
to respect women
when no one made me feel worst
than you ever did
how could you tell our daughter
not to chase boys
when you make me chase you

you can't be the one
this can't be it

I'm still waiting
for someone who treats me right
to come along

I'm stubborn
and I will wait
for my fairy tale

I can't wait
for you to fall in love

to watch as you transform yourself
and become the best version of you
because you can finally see yourself
through loving and wanting eyes
for you to see what I already see
someone to spend a lifetime with
someone whose company makes time fly

I can't wait till you fall in love
and that special someone
gives back to you
what you give to everyone else

showing you care
being interested
wanting something
and going after it
can be
so attractive

pretending not to care
isn't cool
owning up to how you feel
is

comparing
yourself to others
can be deadly

however
admiring others
is not

learn to know
the difference

they say we're like flowers
to each their own beauty
a tulip wouldn't want
the petals of the sunflower

I don't want to be beautiful
like you
I want to be beautiful
like me

I learn from you
how to bloom
in my own way

we're too many
too many girls
afraid to say what happened
tormented by hands on our skin
paralyzed at the sight of someone
frightened by hearing a name

it shouldn't be like this
it won't be like this
slowly but surely
we'll find our voice

I used to cringe
when I was told
I acted like my father

but just as I've learned
to be soft with myself
I'm learning
to be soft with him

"you like because
you love in spite of"
I don't ignore the bad
I just admire the good

I'm proud to be half of him
that's where get my tough outside from
I also get my gooey inside
I get the spite to prove people wrong
I get the need to be better
I get the thirst to want to know more

I couldn't be prouder
than when they tell me
how much
I'm like my father

you can really re-educate yourself
just as you learn you can un-learn
you don't have to be
who you were brought up to be

you're not the circumstances
that surround you
you're the choices you make

you're perfectly capable
of training yourself
to let go of nasty habits
to do better and to be better

there's courage in us all
we just have to be brave enough
to want to change

thank you
for loving me
when I didn't know how to

thank you
for taking the time
to get to know me
when I felt
nobody else wanted to

there's nothing quite
like feeling appreciated

I hope you know
what you've done for me
you seeing me
made me see myself

today I'm able to love myself
because you loved me first

If I could sum up in one word
what this world needs
it would be
empathy

we need to be able to look at others
and realize that it could've been us
in the same exact situation

we didn't choose
where we were born
it was sheer luck

the person going through hell
could've been me
could've been you

the day we all realize that
will maybe be the day
this world
will know peace

I hope you notice
when you admire nature
that you're part of it

you're just as breathtaking
as strong as a river
as beautiful as clouds
as rich as a jungle
as determined as the ocean
as exotic as a bird
as energetic as lightning
as tough as a mountain

nature is part of you
as you are a part of nature
you're just as amazing
as everything that surrounds you

I try to convince myself
I'm not into you
I get crushes all the time
this one too shall pass
the only problem
is that it's been a while

ignoring it
didn't work
the thought of you
is now ever present
in my mind

do you see me in a crowd
and think "oh there she goes"

does your heart leap
out of your chest
does it take a minute
to get back to your own head

is your reaction to seeing me
the same as mine
when seeing you

I'm so excited
for the person I'll become
I've come so far
in so little time

I came out triumphantly
from a place I didn't see
a way out of

I can't wait for who I'll be
it's a never-ending process
that hasn't ceased to amaze me

I can't wait to see how I'll grow
how I'll come out
of whatever life throws at me

how I'll react to different situations
how I'll be able to transform
into someone
that will leave a mark
everywhere I go
and on everyone I meet

and so I find it
I find the courage
to walk up to you
and tell you

because the thought
of you not knowing
doesn't let me sleep

what if I died today
and you never got to know
how I feel

if I never got to know
if you feel it too
and because I can't sleep
I walk up to you
but all that comes out
is a simple "hi"

because greater than the courage
is the fear
the fear of making a fool of myself
the fear of you
not feeling the same way

I stopped using ugly as an insult. actually, I stopped using it as an insult to describe physical traits. beauty is subjective, more than that, beauty is so much more than what can only be seen. beauty cannot be reduced to something so little as a thing that can only be perceived through the eyes. beauty – is felt, transmitted, palpable through all the senses. from now on, when I say someone is ugly, I don't mean they don't look good, I mean they are ugly. there's nothing worse than being ugly on the inside, to emit a negative energy that obscures even physical beauty. the prettier on the inside, the more it reflects on the outside, and vice versa. it took me a long time to realize it, my mom used to say it all the time and only until now I've understood. she used to tell me "do you see how some people age gracefully and some don't? it's not because of skin care, it's because the beauty that really matters, beauty on the inside, is the only one that withstands the passing of time."

you think you're winning
cause you seem emotionless
cause it looks like you don't care

you think you're playing a game
and you got the lead

but you got it all wrong
the ones that don't say how they feel
lose

cause even though love isn't a game
there comes a loss
from the lack of what isn't said

it leaves people with what if's
and the eternal doubt
of what could've been

you like me
I like you

it's as simple
and complicated
as that

I think I might die
if I get the courage to tell you
if I spill my heart out to you
and you tell me thanks
but no thanks

pride will be the end of us
I won't admit I was wrong
you won't say that you're sorry

but this silence between us
and what we don't say to each other
makes more noise than anything else

I should be over there
or you should be over here
the point is
we should be
in each other's arms

you were amazing before he came
before he noticed
you will continue to be amazing
now that he's left

it might not feel like it right now
but the sun will shine again
it's okay if it takes some time
but eventually you'll shine again

may you use your time on earth
to make a positive impact

may you use your talent
to make the world a better place

may you leave this planet
a little better than how you found it

may you touch as many souls
as you possible can

I think I figured out
how to stop being
head over heels for you
more than figured out
I think I realized
that I'm not in love with you

I'm intoxicated with the idea of you
you're not a damaged soul I can fix
you're just a lost boy
trying on girls like they're sweaters
you're not broken and in need of a savior
you're just a foolish kid
that I tried to picture as a man

let her know right now
get out of your own head
stop thinking she'll say no
stop being scared of greatness

your existence on earth is finite
do things that make you feel infinite
feel your pulse race as you tell her
you dream of her only

feel your life transform into forever
when you hear her laugh
feel your existence get lighter
when you finally hold her hand

time is fleeting and we're all dying
you need to stop acting like you're not

I'm pretty sure
that during this lifetime
I found you sooner

you see I made you a promise
that in the next lifetime
we'd be together longer
and the way I'm drawn to you
can only be explained like this

I'm an ever-transforming energy
that has a promise to keep
to her one and only soulmate

and I think it's crazy
how every one of my thoughts
circle back to you
from what I'll wear
to what I'll do

I'm constantly looking forward
to the next time we meet
and when I'm not thinking about you
I'm thinking about us
and what we would be doing
if we were together

I was so so so foolish
for thinking I belonged in your arms
for going against my best instincts
and trying to make a home out of you

for ignoring my mother
when she said you were not the one
and that you should've brought me peace
not frustration and tears

I didn't actually see you
I saw who I thought you would become
I saw the potential
that you never managed to live up to

and while trying to fix you
I ended up breaking myself

where does one draw the line
between not settling
and asking for too much

I'm afraid I'll end up alone
but I'm also terrified
of only knowing mediocre love

of not getting to experience
the type of love
I see around me

I want a "shout from the rooftop"
kind of love
not a "we've-agreed-to-be-together
because-what-if-nothing-better-comes-along"
type of love

if your confidence changes
depending on who you're with
then your self esteem
doesn't belong to you
it belongs to them

I'm like a fountain
that never turns off
I'm so filled with love and life
it overflows

only this time
it doesn't leave me empty

the sadness and the anger
only last a couple hours
and even on my worst days
I laugh and I smile

I'm grateful for finally getting here
not a place where there is no sadness
but a place where the happiness
outweighs all else

it's true
you do have to suck it up
you have to deal with the things
life keeps throwing at you

but it's okay
if one day
you don't feel like
sucking it up

it's okay
if today
isn't the day to suck it up

there's time for everything
and while you can't just give up
on everything you want

it's okay take a day
to rest
to feel powerless
to cry
to feel hopeless

believe me
it's okay
you don't always have
to suck it up

I think
the key to happiness
is gratefulness

the grass will always be greener
on the other side
if we're more worried
with the neighbor's grass
than we are of our own garden

the grass may be greener
but you might have the oak tree
he so desperately wants

if neither is grateful
for what they have
they will always look for happiness elsewhere
when it is clearly growing
within their reach

it's okay if you don't relate
to being broken

we are part of a culture
that romanticizes
self-doubt
and anxiety
and depression

it's okay to be the happy human
don't try to feel broken
it's not the same as sad

just because everyone around you
seems to be going through something
it doesn't mean you have to

be the happy healthy human
and don't apologize for it

screw the girl who made you feel
like you weren't pretty
screw the boy who was embarrassed
when you talked about what you like
screw those that laugh
when you can't get something right

I know
you feel like disappearing
but stop running away from those
who seek to hurt you

confront them
and call them out
make them take a look in the mirror
and be disgusted by what they see

make them feel bad about hurting you
about hurting others
because they really don't deserve
to be at peace with who they are

you're not eager to die
you're eager to live

you don't want to be insignificant
and you're terrified you won't live up
to the life you imagined

but the life you visualize for yourself
is waiting for you
you just need to want it bad enough

instead of being scared
of what you'll miss out on
be curious for what you won't

you don't have to be adventurous
every single day
you just have to be able
to appreciate everything for what it is
and stop wishing it was something else

and I can try all I want
but anyone else
isn't you

I can search for your kiss
on someone else's lips
but I won't succeed

you're one in a billion
and to have touched you
was a once in a lifetime
kind of experience

one of the hardest
but most helpful things
you'll learn to do
is accept
that not everything
has to mean something

I don't want to call it rape
it sounds so awful
and you know honestly
I wasn't forced to do anything
but you took something from me

I don't even believe
in the concept of virginity or purity
but you never asked me if I wanted to
I didn't say no, but I don't think
that my opinion would've mattered

it's taken me a very long time
to realize that it wasn't my fault
I didn't ask for it
just because I was drunk

and now that I know
I'm taking back what you took from me
I'm doing it by calling you out
but also by forgiving you
this is the moment you stop being
someone relevant in my story
It makes me sad to think I'm not the only girl
stripped of something that was hers

but I still hope
you have trouble sleeping at night
and I hope just the same happens
for every person that is just like you

it breaks my heart
to not know what's hurting you so bad
that all you do is lash out at me

it makes me so sad
to not be able to help you
when I feel like your words
are a cry for help

I'm supposed to be there for you unconditionally
but every time you get mad at me
I feel like I've failed

you're like a sculpture
both physically and metaphorically

you're made of stone
with features that seem to have been
carved by Rodin himself
but you're also cold and unreachable
something so beautiful and admirable
that must be seen from afar

I need you to know
that you can show me what's inside
without me needing to use a hammer

I was confused by how I felt
but now I'm relieved

you were obviously not the one
I had been waiting for

I don't have to give up
the meaningful conversation I crave
I don't have to make myself small
because I was afraid I'd scare you away

I'd caught the love bug
I wanted a relationship so bad
and you were the best candidate
the moment's highest bidder

I trust that what's mine will find me

you most obviously
were not mine
as I
am not yours

I called my best friend
told her what you did to me
you didn't just break my heart
you broke her's too

and so people call me a dreamer
thinking it's an insult
insinuating I should be a realist

but no thank you
you see it's us
the dreamers
who will change the world

while others sit and complain
about what is
we'll be visualizing what could be
what will be

there's a Mexican saying
"clavo saca a otro clavo"
(nail takes out another nail)

meaning
the next person that comes along
makes you forget
about the last
or you use a new one
to eventually forget about the old one

but I don't know why
I haven't been able to
I could've gone through the whole toolbox
and I still wouldn't have found a way
to get you out of my head
or is it my heart?

I can't take you out
not with another nail
or even with a hammer

I don't even think
I could get you out
by drilling a hole into my skull

I love reading about love
I can feel my heart smile
and sigh
longing for the love
we both crave

adults need to learn the difference
between knowing what's best
and completely discrediting
the way young people feel

you ask where my lips have been
I ask you where have yours
you laugh and say it's not the same

I ask you why
and you reply with what you believe
is the best thing you've heard
"a key that opens any door
is a master key
a door that is opened by any key
is a faulty door"

and so it hits me
I'm in front of another idiot
who didn't get proper education
who doesn't seem to understand
that what he is saying
objectifies women
that without realizing it
he's calling women holes

nothing will ever change
if men can't stop seeing
women as doors
and themselves as keys

and so I've been both
the brick and the window pane
I've broken somebody
and I've also been hurt
and all I can say
is that I'd rather be the window pane

maybe I feel too much
maybe I care too deeply
maybe for my own sake
I should be more selfish

but I can't live with myself
knowing I tarnished
someone's idea of love
thinking I might be the reason
someone pushes everyone away

the idea that I hurt someone
brings tears to my eyes
and guilt forms in my throat
making it hard
for me to breathe

it's calling for you
your passion
who you're meant to be
what you're meant to do

I hope it doesn't take a life time
for you to figure out
how to hear it

cause when you do
you'll feel your bones vibrate
desperate for you to chase it
you'll feel your heart jump
at the idea of it coming true
you'll feel your feet restless
eager to take you all the way

you dream of angels
the presence of a celestial being
you want ethereal and white wings
someone to be your light
and your salvation

but you're looking in the wrong place
like the angels
I'm also out of this world
only instead
I'm a burning sun
a shooting star
I crash only to be born again

I don't bring salvation
I bring destruction
I'll help you burn to ashes
only for you to be reborn

instead of heaven I'll take you to space
where we can hold hands on the moon
and dance in the milky way

I won't save you
but maybe
I'll help you save yourself

we're all going to become a number one day. person number 756,354 to die of old age due to heart failure. person number 3,000,027 to die from kidney failure. person 234,889 to die from lung cancer. we're going to become statistics and pie charts in science school books. we might as well be more than a number, we might as well do something extraordinary. by extraordinary I don't mean make a discovery, or invent something new, or become rich or famous or powerful. I mean be extraordinary, with a whole other meaning. be the person that prevents another person from becoming number 1,345,853 from people that die from suicide. be a person that spends money they spare on a foundation that funds free education. be a person that uses their platform to raise awareness and do good. be a person that is kind to other humans, and plants and animals too. be a person that spends a summer in a beach, helping clean the ocean and restore corals. be a person that does an act so kind, the newspaper headlines are positive for at least one day. be a person that can be proud to have brought light into what most think is darkness.

some people are like dawn
a new beginning
to a heavy night

the promise of sunshine
the tenderness of light
somethings so bright
it warms others up

I know I'm made of energy
when the only word I can think of
to describe your touch is electric

I know I'm 70% water
when your smile
causes waves inside me

I know I have particles of moon dust
when my longing for you
is out of this world

I think the key is to have both
to not have to choose
between one or the other

the love of today's morning
the lust of last night

things are destined to end
as soon as they start
the sun starts to set
the moment it rises

but instead of having
to choose between
day and night

you can have a little of both
having both the love and the lust
would mean you get the sun
and also the stars

I like to think that I'm the artist
I have a way with words
to describe you
like no one else can

but I think
I underestimated you

the way my body unfolds to your touch
has got to be art too

I've always loved the idea
of being someone's muse
to have someone
write a song about me
or want to paint me

but I am something much greater
I'm the paintbrush you use
I'm the instrument you play

your lovemaking to me
is the art I get to be
and experience

and so I realize
that even though
we're under the same moon
it doesn't mean a damn thing

cause I look up at it
and think of you looking at it
and visualizing me too
but you probably don't even look at it
you're probably caught up
in something else
maybe you're even thinking
about someone else too

and so I don't
I don't longer find comfort
in looking at the same moon
or sleeping under the same stars

what I do find is relief
from finally being free
of this consuming habit
of wanting you to want me

she shines
even though
she's broken
and that
is magic

I'd say loving you
was a waste of time
but it wasn't

it brought darkness
and it brought tears
but it made me realize
you're everything
I don't want
you're everything
I'll try to avoid in the future

and most important of all
I'm capable of finding light
within myself
to outshine the darkness
others like you might bring

I said you'd gotten under my skin
as a figure of speech
as a way of saying
you make me tick where others can't

but you got under my skin
and now there's no getting you out
you're etched into my bones
where I can't wash or drink you away

you're in so deep
I can't ask my heart to forget you
it already tries
because it knows you're poison to me
I also can't ask my mind
because it's already tried
to replace your name with others

you're so far gone
none of us can get you out

I like the way
she wears her beauty
like pearl earrings
or a silver bracelet

she wears it in the shower
and at night in bed
she wears her beauty
and never takes it off

and because I wear
my heart on my sleeve
I also keep it on a leash

because if I were ever
to let go
it would wander to you
like a lost dog

looking for a way back
to where it belongs
looking for a place
to call home

we make a great mistake
when it comes to relationships
we have this fantasy
that it's either a forever love
or a tragic end type of love
we think it'll happen
just as it does in books and movies

but the tragic part
is that it won't be tragic

one will fall out of love
or lose interest
or change their minds
and decide to leave
with no explanations
and unanswered questions
left behind

you don't choose
who you fall in love with

but you do get to choose
when to leave
if you're not treated right

I've tried to picture myself
as the soft girl
to think I wear flowers on my head
to believe I can be nice to everyone
and acknowledge their opinions
and understand their feelings

but I can't
I'm not the soft girl
I wear poisonous leaves, an Ivy crown
I call people out on their bullshit
and stand for what I think is right

the world needs
more girls who wear ivy crowns
and who light up the world
calling out and fighting injustice

it's such a shame
we always seem
to be looking at each other

it's such a same
because there's something there
but neither of us
seems to have the courage
to find out what it is

and so all we do
is look each other's way

and please
as you rip me apart
be gentle with me

you will rip me apart
it's unavoidable

I'm just asking you
to take your time

don't get to know her
don't find out what's underneath
'cause you'll never be able to leave

the curated version of herself
is only what she lets other see
she was told too many times
that perhaps she was too much
and so she hides it all

if you try to crack the hard shell
you'll find the treasure underneath
a treasure so compelling
you'll never be able to look away
a place like paradise
you'll never want to leave
a chaos so mesmerizing
all you'll want to do
is melt into it

I think I may have killed
the possibility of us
with all this thinking and daydreaming

I imagined so much potential
I'm afraid we wouldn't be able
to live up to it

I turned the reality into a false ideal
that no one'll reach

the love story I imagined
belongs only on paper

untarnished
unrealized

they say it's a battle
between the heart and the head
what I think
and what I feel

but what happens
when they both agree

when the person in front of me
is willing to give me everything
but I also wouldn't mind
if he didn't offer it

am I so damaged
I can't recognize healthy love
staring me in the face
or did I read too many books
and I'm waiting for something
that will never come

I think you'd fall in love with yourself
if you were actually the person
I idealized you to be

you'll be searching your whole life
for someone to look at you
the way I did

you'll pray all your life
to come across someone
that thinks about you the way I thought I did

I built you a shrine
I made you a religion
but the only devoted follower was me

and now I'm gone

it's not that I don't care any more
it's that I don't know if you do

and while I have no control
over the way you feel
I'm taking control
over the way I do

cause unfortunately
all this wishing and hoping
seems to lead
to nowhere

I wish I was pushing you away
thinking I'm damaged and I'll hurt you
thinking I'm not good enough for you
but I know it's not either

It's not self-sabotage
it's fear
fear of a mediocre love
fear of a life lacking passion
scared of this being it

and while I'm giving up
the chance to feel appreciated
I will not give up
my idea of love

self-care is
owning up to who you are
and what you do
it's taking responsibility
for your actions

while it is taking time
to take care of yourself

it is also making the effort
and trying your best
of being the best possible version
of the person you can be

"grow into it" they say

but what can become of the flower
if the seed was planted with guilt
and it was watered with miscommunication
and the sun shone but not for it
(it only shone for itself)

a flower can't grow in these conditions
only a poisonous guilt-driven vine

she goes through men
like she goes through books:
at different paces

but in the end
she devours them all
when she finishes one
it's on to the next

she collects them all
piles them up
remembers them dearly
but she's in the constant search
of one that she'll like more

a better plot
a better character
a better ending

the heat of the beach
the coolness of the pool
the sound of the waves
the moonlight on my skin

the perfect moment

and while I was floating
starring at the stars in the sky
all I could think
was that their brightness
can't compare
to the sparkle in your eyes
whenever you smile

and he said
she's art with legs
and the other answered
'she belongs in a museum'
where men can admire her
for all the time to come

and so I pictured her
like art

as a painting in a museum in New York
in a room next to Degas' Ballerinas
or as a sculpture in Rome
located in the middle of a plaza
or announced with her own exposition
at the Grand Palais in Paris

with the picture I made in my head
I too would've fallen for her

and so I laid there
five am

tired from the long night
that was transitioning into the day
wishing I could go to sleep

but how could I
when there are cotton candy skies
how could I close my eyes
knowing there was such beauty

was it selfish to believe
God had hand painted the sky
only for me?

you make me tingle in places
I haven't tingled before

instead of feeling butterflies
in my stomach
I tingle all over

in my hands
on the left side of my chest
between my legs
in the tips of my toes

my friend got out of your car
with your skin under her nails
and tears in her eyes
bruises on her body
and your taste in her mouth

my friend got out of your car
wanting to scream
but only managing to cry instead
wanting the earth to swallow her whole
and instead had to walk home

so no
you weren't just messing around
she didn't exaggerate what happened
you weren't just enjoying the moment
she didn't get scared over nothing

you tried taking something
that was never yours to take
you abused of someone
you deemed weaker than you
but take a long look in the mirror
the one with no balls is you

I can't see you in my dreams anymore
I used to want to fall asleep
so I could see you every night
and not just when we bump into each other
but it's been some days now
and you don't come to me anymore

I think you're in someone else's dream now
because I can't find you in mine
I hope the person dreaming of you
also gets to wake up next to you

I hope to them you're not an illusion
or a fantasy of what could be
but never was

love

what sweet song
what sad ballad
along with the high
always comes the withdrawal

there's no thing as too much
one can't overdose on love
the high won't kill you
but the withdrawal might

I think I'll remember us like this
a short incomplete tragedy

I won't remember what we were
I'll remember what we couldn't be
which is everything

fireworks
poems
grand gestures
and love songs

that's what it'll be
an untarnished image
of something that was so close
to come to life

come darling
come lay with me
we won't make love
love will make us

it's still not enough
you and me
all tangled up in bed
our fingers intertwined
skin on skin
nose against nose

being this close
is still not enough
for how close
I want to be to you

with privilege
comes responsibility

the greater your advantages
(either economical or educational)
the harder you must work
for those who have less

you have the obligation
to make your voice heard
to speak for those
who are unable to

it's a self-preservation thing
calling boys
"flavor of the month"
anticipating their unavoidable flee
or my tendency to push them away

he bottled me up
believing he'd caught lightning
thinking I'd be a flash of light
in his dark days
an entertainment for
his lonely nights

bur darling
with lightning comes the storm
my laugh may sometimes be
a shock of happiness and electricity
but the storm is dark
it destroys everything
chews it up and then spits it out

I don't heal, I tear up
he should know
the few moments of happiness
won't make up
for what comes after that

can one seriously
look at the sky
pink
blue
orange
purple
all the colors in between
and not believe in magic?

I like to feel your eyes on me
as I look away
and pretend not to notice

don't let yourself get boxed up
as if you're a gift
that needs to be wrapped up

don't give into society's constant need
to put a label on everything
you don't have to defined
solely by one thing

you can be kind to everyone
and mean to whoever crosses you
you can like sports
and also fashion
you can be a book worm
and a party animal too
you can be a romantic
and also a realist

all the things you like
don't define you
humans aren't something to be defined
or caged up

we're rather something to be admired
and appreciated
exactly for what we are

letting go
of reality
is easy

what is hard
is letting go
of dreams

most lovers go
through the same stages
a dream
a reality
then a memory

the problem
with being so emotional
so all or nothing
so black and white
is that when you're done with someone
you're done with them forever

true friendship
is a rare and magical thing
it's hard to come by
and if you're really lucky
you'll be able to count them
with both hands

most of your friendships
will come with expiration dates
they're people who come with a lesson
but are also just temporary
and because of this
don't feel obligated
to connect with everyone

wait for those really special people
that will complete you
in things you didn't know
you were lacking

it's easier to be angry
it takes courage
to be sad
to accept you have a broken heart
to realize your spirit has been crushed

I promise to be in love with you
the way I'm in love with the sky

when it's a mix of orange and pink
like it was hand painted by the gods

when it's grey and gloomy
like a warning for a storm

when it's clear and blue without a cloud
giving a feeling of serenity

when it's dark during night-time
and scares people away

I find it hard to be an atheist
when I swear
I found God on your lips

and our kiss
felt celestial
because I heard heaven sing

so what do I do? when I can't imagine myself tied to one place, but I want your arms to be what I call home. when I don't like explaining myself to others, but I want you to understand me. what should I give into? I'm a contradicting mess who wants to be loved but would rather die than be tamed.

envision it
what you wish your life was
being so caught up in the what you do
you have no time for self-pity
nor feeling hopeless or defeated
after a bad day

having an unknown feeling
where all you want to do
is shout "no bad days" from a rooftop
being able to give your parents
everything they deserve
finally taking that trip you dream of
and financing it yourself
waking up next to the love of your life
and getting to hop in the shower with them too

because that's how you get
to your dream life
envisioning it
wanting it so much
you can almost taste it

having tasted it
willing to stop at nothing
to get it all
because it's waiting for you
all you have to do
is be determined to work for it

even if I'm in a rush
or if my world is upside down
it brings me peace
it makes me serene

I like to think of it
as my paradise

I get the same feeling
as if I woke up by the beach
the sound of the waves
the smell of the salt
the warmth of the sun
the breeze on my skin

eye contact and your kiss
is all I need

it's my calm between the storm
it's what makes my world stop
no matter what's chaos
is going on

it's not an awful world
we make it an awful world

we have to own up
to our actions
maybe that way
we'll become conscious
that it's our responsibility

the world works
with cause and effect
not just "because"

so no
the world isn't an awful place
we make it an awful place

and while some things
are out of our control or our reach
we owe it to humanity
to do and be the best we can
with the people and the space around us

would you accept the love
I'm willing to give to you
even if you didn't come first?

I'm already committed to someone else
I'm already devoted to life itself
so I could only take you as my lover

as a partner on my constant adventure
forever chasing the one
I already love

I think I should learn morse code
see, she speaks to me with her eyes
holding a gaze that can drive me insane

and when she blinks
I feel a secret message
sent just to me

I should definitely learn morse code
she speaks to me through eye-blinks
and when I close my eyes
all I can see are eyelashes
and coffee colored eyes

clinging to your shoulder blades
is where I'm highest

there's nowhere I'd rather be
than between your arms
not being sure
where you end
and I begin
becoming one
under the bed sheets

I have seen the light
and devoted myself
to a new religion

poetry is
me waking up
in the middle of the night
because I finally found
words to describe you
that do you justice

I desperately need
a breath of fresh air

but how can I breathe
when you're away
and you're the air I need
to fill my lungs

you're not next to me
and I can hardly breathe

you make me
dream about you
in technicolor

and so I loved you
relentlessly
and without agenda
with all your flaws
and all your qualities

but when I took a step back
when I stopped loving you
I realized your flaws
did more damage
than your love
could ever make up for

it's so sad
how the most damage
done to womanhood
can sometimes be done by women

fear about what men might say
makes us turn on each other
we sometimes judge one another
more harshly than men do

when we insult other women
we insult ourselves
we must get past this pettiness
of competing against each other
for approval no one asked for
and no man values

It's not a fight against men
it's a fight for acceptance
between women
it's a fight for the realization
we're stronger
when we lift each other up
than when we tear each other down

by putting you on a pedestal
you ended up being
too far away for me to reach

I wonder if it gets lonely up there
people staring in awe
but never coming close enough
for any contact at all

it's not a right
it's an obligation
just as you were entitled
to freedom and education

it's your obligation to humanity
to do whatever you can
to help others obtain
what you got for free

you are responsible for fighting
for those who can barely fight
because they don't have
the means or the tools

you are obligated to raise your voice
for those that don't have one
for those afraid to use it
because they might get killed

as humans we have an obligation
an unwritten pact to help each other
to do everything in our power
to fight against injustice

open yourself up to me
show me who you truly are
and I promise
I'll start a fire within you
that will keep you warm
even after I'm gone

while chasing a meteorite
she came across a star
and it took her breath away

she realized
she had been chasing someone
headed for their own destruction

instead

she decided to go after someone
who shone their light on her
and ignited one within in herself

I want to pretend
like you calling at 3am
is irrelevant

but it's been three weeks
and I'm a little tipsy

I'm staring at my phone
and the impulse to call you
is stronger than my will not to

I remembered I used to love you
I remembered I still do

something out of this world
in the way
you move
and carry yourself

it's almost indescribable
something beyond beautiful

in loving you
and the way
you love me back

last night
I told the moon
what I would do to you

it sighed so loud
and shone so bright
that night the tide
was higher than it'd ever been

complete and utter ecstasy

like you're going too fast
and you know you should hit the brakes
cause you're not in control
and you might crash
but instead going faster
cause nothing's ever made you feel more alive
and you've never been so high
completely surrendering control
of the direction you're heading in
but holding on like your life depends on it
because in this exact moment
it does

greater than the fear
of not trying
or trying and failing

is the fear
of being unremarkable
or feeling your presence
replaceable

those who are truly happy
live immersed
in the object
of their contemplation

I think
I lose friendships
as time passes by
because I'm making space
for people who will come along
and actually be worth it

I need to make space
for these all-consuming people
that bring along all-consuming love

the older I grow
the better I understand
"quality over quantity"

I'd rather invest time in five people
over twenty
if it means I'm a priority for them too

I had it all planned
all figured out

the things to come
were all lined up
experiences
people
emotions

I had it all figured out
but everything turned upside down
when you decided to cut in line

be kind
not because others need it
but because you do

letting you go
and pushing you away
was the most selfless thing I could do
cause you wouldn't leave
even though I was bad for you

you were like a spaceship
eager to get close to the sun
consumed by my uniqueness
not realizing
you were melting away

I like you
but I don't like you enough
for you to ruin me

I'm not going all in
without knowing I have
a winning hand

it's not a sacrifice
I'm willing to make
not for you anyway

and so I wake up
and thank God
that when I tried to call you last night
I didn't find your number

I don't thank God
I thank you
for not giving me a way
to reach out to you

maybe you don't realize it
but you helped me
and prevented
any further damage

and now that people only see
what I want them to see
the only thing I crave
is someone who won't be fooled

you'll see me everywhere

in your daughter
when she answers back
and you see in her
the same fire
you saw in me

in your morning coffee
before you take your time
to pour in too much milk
because you don't see coffee
you see the color of my eyes

in the laugh of a woman
across the room
and you'll know it's not mine
but you spend too much time
wishing it were

in strangers
when you think
that every tall brunette with long hair
you see from behind
is me

in your dreams
and when you close your eyes
and all you see are white sheets
and lace
and me mouthing I love you

I know you'll see me
everywhere
the same way I see you
everywhere

you'll come to find
that most of the people
who demand an explanation
don't actually deserve one

feel entitled to only explain yourself
to the people you deem worthy

have you seen the female body?
really looked at it?
appreciated it?

It looks carved by the gods
more beautiful than anything
on this earth

don't you dare disrespect it
or try to enter it with permission

wrapped up in each other
that's the most accurate description
there could ever be
for how we should always be

one day I'll be old
my kidney will be failing
I may find it hard to walk
but I would still be able to tell you
about the one I loved

the shape of their nose
what they tasted like
the exact color of their eyes
what their first words where to me
the way they smelled
what they were wearing when we met
the sound of their laugher

I'll remember them
the same way
anyone remembers
how to ride a bicycle

I don't believe
anything brings people closer
than an afternoon
of sharing tales
of lost love

I know now
you're the one
and I swear to you this

from now on
wherever you go
I'll go too

I find myself again
in this not so strange place
actually
in this all too familiar place

the darkness
takes over my life again
and I find comfort

it had become so trying
the light
the happiness
the smiling

I find relief in letting go
in being consumed by the darkness

I find peace
the pressure is gone
and the lack of light is visible

I become the image of disappointment
and the expectations
become strangers
once again

and I know now
that you weren't the one for me
but if only you knew
how many nights I spent
wishing you had been

leaving you behind
was like dropping dead weight
you only slowed me down
on my path to where I needed to be

for so long
I had wanted you to love me
that I wouldn't know what to do
if you actually said you did

are you trying to forget me
or did you cover me up
do you constantly make an effort
to get over me
or do you distract yourself
with anything that comes up

do you do all this
only to remember me
with a song that comes up
or at the bottom of the bottles
you drown in every weekend

I can't help but smile
and feel relieved

you broke me
because someone else
had broken you

there was never
something wrong with me

all along, all this time
what was wrong
was you

I don't know

if I should find comfort
in knowing I was only used
and it had nothing to do with me

or if I should feel sad
over not being enough
to make you forget about her

I hope her smile
lights you up
contrary to mine
which you pretended to ignore

I hope when she's goofing around
you join her
rather than doing what you did to me
all those sighs and eye rolls

but most of all
I hope she sees her worth
I hope she knows when to leave
if she's not treated right

she's not my enemy for being
the one for you
she's my ally for seeing what I saw
and trying to love you despite it all

she broke you
you broke me
I'm about to break him

I want to
just to know how it feels
to break
and not to feel broken

but I owe it to myself
the girl that cried over you
and I owe it to him
who was nothing but kind
to end this right here

to not participate
in this chain of hurt

it kinda stings
hurts actually

to know that you didn't hurt me
trying to put yourself back together

you hurt me with the sole purpose
of hurting her
of entertaining yourself
and trying to forget her

I'd been removing
toxic people from my life
for quite some time now
but somehow
I always clung on to you

I bullshitted a bullshitter
I made excuses
and told myself
it was the right thing to do
I lied when I said that putting up with you
didn't drain me

maybe I felt guilty
for not loving you back

but even though I feel the need
to be there for you
my mental health
comes before yours

you were an inconvenience
but you then became a burden
and carrying us both
ended up being too much for me

you don't cross my mind
a hundred times a day
you came in one day
and never left

there are poems
just waiting to happen

in everything I touch
and see
and feel
and read

all floating in the air
waiting for me
to put them in paper

I made a list
of pros and cons
of the ways you filled me
and the ways you drained me

but I'd wasted my time
the fact I had to make a list
was already a warning sign
people aren't lists

I know I shouldn't carry
all this baggage
I know I shouldn't bring it along
but I do

I want to get on
our little love boat
and sail away
where no one else matters

but I'm afraid
the boat would sink
with all this baggage
I carry with me

I want to throw it overseas
but it's become a part of me
I've been carrying it so long
I consider them limbs

when I try to leave it behind
I feel like something's missing
and while I'm dying to get on our boat
I think I need someone with a ship

I'm dying to know
why you call me
I'm dying to ask
but I won't

cause as our story goes
I won't ask
and you won't explain

and so it goes
our pride got the best of us
you
me
we're both to blame

but I'm dying to know
why you call
I refuse to ask
so I can only assume

are you so drunk
you can't think straight
and all you remember
is the way you feel about me

do you crave my touch
or just anybody's
do you want my lips
or just anybody's

do you really miss me
or did no one catch your eye tonight
would you be calling
if a pretty girl had looked your way

I'm dying to know
but I won't lose sleep over it
I'm dying to know
but I think I'll never know

a common problem we have
is that when we feel lost
we don't look for ourselves within us

we look for ourselves in others
and we stray away from the path
of coming back to ourselves

I want to run
the last time I felt like this
pieces of me
ended up everywhere

I hurt so bad
I didn't know anything but pain
I couldn't see beyond
the sadness that swallowed me whole

(I'm sorry if I run)

all of us looking up
at the same thing
picturing
such different things

mesmerized by the magic

content with someone besides us
or longing
for the person we wish
were beside us

— blood moon

I'm engulfed by it
the smell of us

your lotion
my perfume
our sweat
your bedsheets
the fresh air
the cigarette in your hand

this smell of us
is forever
impregnated in my mind
it's now become a permanent memory
to my senses

it can ruin you
loving someone
who doesn't appreciate you

it's being seen
and having someone else deciding
it's not good enough

you tear down you walls to let them in
only to have to build them back up
all by yourself

even though
I haven't met you
I already know
I belong to you

tell me what's on your mind
spill out your heart
I'll help you carry
whatever's making you feel heavy

I'll hold up the ceiling
you feel is crashing down on you
I'll tear down the walls
you feel are shutting you in

I won't be able to take the pain away
but I'll always be there
to try and make you laugh
or hug you until you don't feel blue

there's nothing more inspiring
than the beaming moon
shining amidst the darkness
of the (sometimes heavy) night

those of us that find comfort
in looking up at it
have moondust in our veins
and hope in our hearts

www.ingramcontent.com/pod-product-compliance
Lightning Source LLC
LaVergne TN
LVHW041631060526
838200LV00040B/1535